W.W.WEST

Edited and Compiled
by Carrie L. Compton

First Edition
Published by W.W.West, Inc.
20875 Sholes Road
Bend, Oregon 97702
Book Design by Linda McCray
Illustrations by Dave Ember

ISBN 0-9727921-4-7
Library Catalog data available upon request
Printed in China by C & C Offset Printing Co.

A

Animals

With the successful introduction of the wolf, every animal species living in Yellowstone when the park was created is there today!

The Pronghorn **Antelope** is the fastest animal in Yellowstone, 60 mph for short distances.

A Grizzly, or Bison, can run faster than the fastest human.

B

Bison

In 1900 a survey counted only 25 wild Bison in Yellowstone National Park.

Today, Yellowstone has the largest, and only true wild Bison herd in North America.

C

Coyote

A predator that is very important to keeping Nature's balance in the park.

D

Diversity

E

Elk

By some estimates there are 30,000 Elk living in Yellowstone National Park. Yellowstone has the largest Elk population in the world.

"When do the Elk turn into Moose?"

Tourist question to Park Ranger

F

Firehole River

This river is fed by hot springs and geyser water flow. It never freezes, even in the coldest Yellowstone winters.

G

Geysers

Two-thirds of the world's geysers are in Yellowstone National Park. There are almost 10,000 hot springs, mud pots, steam vents (fumaroles) and geysers in Yellowstone.

Excelsior Geyser/Midway Geyser Basin

Great Fountain Geyser

West Thumb Geyser Basin

Castle Geyser

H

Hayden Valley

This is a great place for summertime viewing of Bison and Elk.

Hayden Valley is named for Ferdinand V. Hayden, who led an 1871 survey expedition mapping and photographing Yellowstone. Hayden recommended to Congress the area be named a public park.

I

Indian Paint Brush

Indian Paint Brush is the Wyoming State Flower. In July, these flowers are in bloom throughout the park.

Only one **Indian** tribe made their home year-round in Yellowstone—a Shoshone band named Sheepeaters.

J

Jeopardy

What is man without the beasts? If all the beasts were gone, men would die from great loneliness of spirit, for whatever happens to the beasts also happens to man.

Chief Seattle

K

Kepler Cascades

We call upon the waters
that rim the earth,
horizon to horizon,

that flow in our rivers
and streams, that fall
upon our fields,

and we ask that they—
Teach us and show us
the way.

Chinook prayer

L

Liberty Cap

"Look up and down and round about you! A thousand Yellowstone Wonders are calling."

John Muir

M

Minerva Terrace

At Mammoth Hot Springs the white rock of Minerva Terrace is formed by flowing, mineral filled waters. The resulting deposit is named travertine.

National Park

In 1872 Yellowstone was the world's first area to be designated as a national park establishing 2.2 million acres of protected wilderness.

We can never have enough of nature.

Henry David Thoreau

O

Old Faithful

Old Faithful is the most famous geyser in Yellowstone, although not the most powerful. Steamboat Geyser , in Norris Geyser Basin, is the world's tallest geyser eruption—300 up to 400 feet into the air.

"**Old Faithful Inn** is as much a part of Yellowstone National Park as the geyser it is named after."

Lee Whittlesey, Park Historian

P

Pelicans

A rookery on Molly Island in Yellowstone Lake, is one of only a few White Pelican breeding places in the world.

Q

Quaking Aspens

There are rainbows in the forest as
leaves respond to autumn's chill. It
seems an artist let a palette spill.

William F. Dittler

R

Rivers

The Yellowstone River is the last major free-flowing river in America.

I have no hesitation in pronouncing the Yellowstone—the best trout-fishing stream on earth.

General William Tecumseh Sherman, 1877

S

Snowfall

A winter visit to Yellowstone National Park can be an adventure. Average snowfall in Yellowstone is 150 inches. In the higher altitudes the snowfall approaches 400 inches some years. However, in the Upper Geyser Basin the winter snowfall average is only 100 inches.

T

Trout Creek

Civilized people are beginning to find out that wilderness is a necessity.

John Muir

U

Ursus Arctos Horribillus
Better known as Grizzly Bear.

When I'm in bear country, I recognize only two kinds of trees—those that I can climb and those that I can't.

Barbara Pettinga, survivor of a grizzly attack.

To a Grizzly Bear almost everything is food, except granite.

John Muir

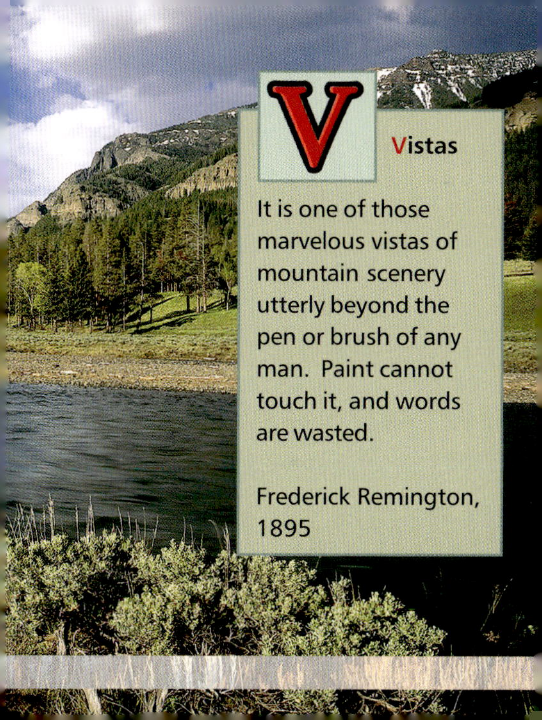

V

Vistas

It is one of those marvelous vistas of mountain scenery utterly beyond the pen or brush of any man. Paint cannot touch it, and words are wasted.

Frederick Remington, 1895

W

Wolves

The prospect of seeing a wolf is "The Holy Grail of Yellowstone Wildlife Sightings."

Paul Schullery, author

X

X-Country Skiing

All the senses are hushed and quieted, the nerves soothed, the soul steeped in the infinite beauty of the scene.

An English Earl traveling Yellowstone in 1874

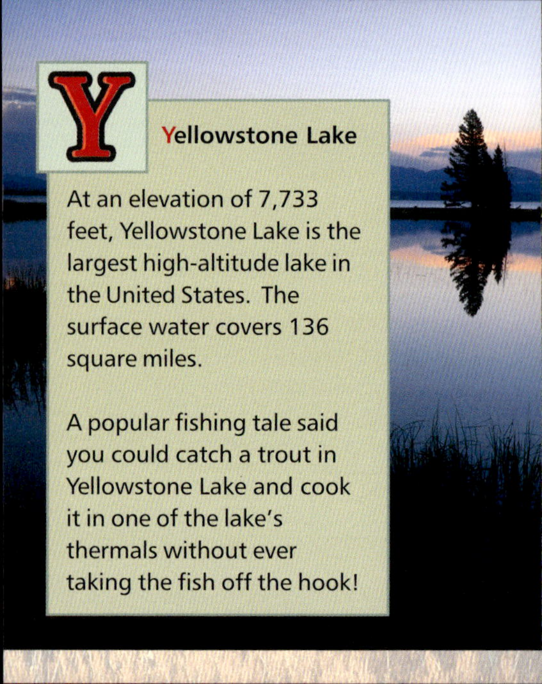

Y

Yellowstone Lake

At an elevation of 7,733 feet, Yellowstone Lake is the largest high-altitude lake in the United States. The surface water covers 136 square miles.

A popular fishing tale said you could catch a trout in Yellowstone Lake and cook it in one of the lake's thermals without ever taking the fish off the hook!

Z — Nez Perce

Nez Perce is one of several Native American tribes that traveled through the Yellowstone area. Led by Chief Joseph they fled to Yellowstone, attempting to escape from the pursuing US Army.

We are content to let things remain as the Great Spirit has made them.

Chief Joseph of the Nez Perce

Sources and Acknowledgements

Chinook—A Native American people who lived along the Columbia River in the Northwest.

William F. Dittler—A retired Presbyterian minister, now writing devotional poetry.

Chief Joseph (1840-1904)—The leader of the Nez Perce during their dramatic attempted escape to Canada from a pursuing U.S. Army.

John Muir (1838-1914)—A conservationist, naturalist, explorer and author who was instrumental in establishing Yosemite as a national park.

Nez Perce—Native American tribe that lived in Northeastern Oregon, Southeastern Washington and parts of Idaho.

Barbara Pettinga—The survivor of a Grizzly attack. Her story is told in Yellowstone Country—*The Enduring Wonder* by Seymour L. Fishbein.

Fred Pflughoft—Watercolor artist turned nature photographer. He is the lead photographer for this Yellowstone gift book series.

Frederick Remington (1861-1909)—U.S. artist and sculptor best known for his works of the American West.

Paul Schullery—Author of many nature books, including *Mountain Time* and *Lewis and Clark among the Grizzlies.*

Chief Seattle (1786-1866)—A leader of the tribes in the Puget Sound, Washington area. He is the most frequently quoted Native American.

William Tecumseh Sherman (1820-1891)—Civil War general famous for his march on Atlanta and then to the sea.

Henry David Thoreau (1817-1862)—U.S. philosopher and author who lived his life captivated by nature's wonders.

Lee Whittlesey—Is Senior Yellowstone Park Historian and author of several books on the park.

Photo Credits

Page	Title
Fred Pflughoft Copyright ©	
2-3	Grand Canyon of Yellowstone River
11	American Bison
16-17	American White Pelican
19	Bull Elk near Canyon Village
20	Firehole River
23	Excelsior Geyser in Midway Basin
24a	Great Fountain Geyser
25a	West Thumb Geyser Basin
26-27	Rainbow over Castle Geyser
28	Yellowstone River in Hayden Valley
30-31	Indian Scarlet Paintbrush
36-37	Kepler Cascades
38-39	Liberty Cap
41	Minerva Terrace at Mammoth Hot Springs
42	Gull Point Cloud Reflections
44	West Thumb Geyser Basin
45	Lower Falls of Yellowstone River
46	Old Faithful Geyser
50-51	Old Faithful Geyser and Inn
52-53	American White Pelican
54	Fall Aspens near Mammoth Hot Springs
56-57	Fall Colors near Elk Creek
58	Yellowstone River in Hayden Valley

60-61 Frosty Sunrise
62-63 Evening Light at Trout Creek
66-67 Soda Butte Creek, in distance Abiathar Peak(L) and Amphitheater Mountain(R)
70-71 X-Country Skiing Upper Geyser Basin
73 Yellowstone Lake from Gull Point
75 Castle Geyser

John C Eriksson Copyright ©

12-13 Coyote Hunting
14a Western Meadowlark

John L. Hinderman Copyright ©

6 Gray Wolf
8 Pronghorn Antelope
14b Gray Wolf
15a Mountain Lion
34a Black Bear
34b Bull Moose
35 Mountain Lion
64 Grizzly Bear
68 Gray Wolf

Montana Historical Society Copyright ©

80 Chief Joseph of Nez Perce

David Morris Copyright ©

4-5 Bull Elk in Madison River
48 Balcony Old Faithful Inn
49 Fireplace in the Great Hall

Chief Joseph of Nez Perce